All the Gold Hurts My Mouth

All the Gold
Hurts My Mouth

KATHERINE LEYTON

icehouse poetry
an imprint of Goose Lane Editions

Edited by David Seymour.
Cover artwork by Kathryn Macnaughton.
Cover and page design by Chris Tompkins.
Printed in Canada.
10 9 8 7 6 5 4 3 2 1

Library and Archives Canada Cataloguing in Publication

Leyton, Katherine, 1983-, author
    All the gold hurts my mouth / Katherine Leyton.

Poems.
Issued in print and electronic formats.
ISBN 978-0-86492-886-3 (paperback). — ISBN 978-0-86492-846-7 (epub). —
ISBN 978-0-86492-847-4 (mobi)

    I. Title.

PS8623.E99A46 2016   C811'.6   C2015-906816-9
                                                 C2015-906817-7

We acknowledge the generous support of the Government of Canada,
the Canada Council for the Arts, and the Government of New Brunswick.

Nous reconnaissons l'appui généreux du gouvernement du Canada,
du Conseil des arts du Canada, et du gouvernement du Nouveau-Brunswick.

Goose Lane Editions
500 Beaverbrook Court, Suite 330
Fredericton, New Brunswick
CANADA E3B 5X4
www.gooselane.com

For Clay

The memory has as many moods as the temper,
and shifts its scenery like a diorama.

— George Eliot, *Middlemarch*

A female human being is born out of her mother's fair
body, branded with a strange, plague-tainted name, and
let go; and lives a while, and dies. But before she dies she
awakes. There is a pain that goes with it.

— Mary MacLane, *I Await The Devil's Coming*

CONTENTS

Richard Gere's Grand Piano 9
I am riding toward an apocalypse —
   I think it's mine. 10
Advertisements 11
Search 12
The First Time with Pay-Per-View 14
Photograph 15
Country Drive 16
Bees 17
The County 18
Rotate 21
Frequencies 22
Letters for You 23
The Misogynist 28
Father's Son 29
Astrocottage 30
Small City 31
Curiosity 32
King West: Brian 34
Trinity Bellwoods Park: Girl 35
Liberty Village: Sepehr 36
Love, Montreal 37
Women-Only Beach, Porto Marina, Egypt 38
Private Tours. Rome. 39
Lower Forms of Life 40
You and I in This House 41
Beaut 46
Instagram 48
Victims 49
Body 50
Witness 54
Margaret Hannah 55
Photograph of Mother 56
Cancer 57
The Council 58
Notes 59
Acknowledgements 61

RICHARD GERE'S GRAND PIANO

Here. This is it:
you're a waitress.
You bring people French toast

and bacon. You can't pay the Hydro bill.
I used to think of you as somebody

grand, like one of those pianos Edward
fucked Vivian on in *Pretty Woman.*

Maybe you are.

Maybe your greatest talent
is gleaming in empty foyers.

I AM RIDING TOWARD AN APOCALYPSE—
I THINK IT'S MINE.

Watch me on my bike.
On Facebook.
On Instagram.

Watch the sun beat through a lawn tree.
I want to go to sleep there and burn

until it is quiet through me like woods,
but even the woods are in perfect rows,
planted by a man in boots,

his back trembling.
I saw him in a documentary.

I call these thoughts death,
but my death is no longer original;
I saw it in a documentary.

You already said that.

ADVERTISEMENTS

TV shows imagine God is listening.
They signal this with synthesized violins.

My idea of the idea of God
is a good ol' boy

in a cardigan, His hands
resting snugly in pockets,

winking at the television,
asking me what I'm selling.

I'm not so sure. We watch a girl
at The Gap fold a sweater. I cup a breast,

measure my waist, and ask God
if my sanity is that sweater, collapsed

in a box with a ribbon around it.
Ahhh, He gasps, *the girls in their Revlon!*

and starts to boogie to the jingle
like a new man.

SEARCH

Type in *girls*
and Google pulls up its skirt:

thumbnail upon thumbnail of cunt

dildo in wet cunt
cellphone in wet cunt
zucchini in wet cunt
Colin Farrell in wet cunt
some kind of mythical creature in wet cunt

big cunt
bare cunt

French cunt
German cunt

vintage cunt
cunt new and improved
cunt like you've never seen before
cunt on the beach
cunt in the forest
cunt on the rocky shores of Labrador

her cunt
your cunt
my cunt

cunt in the dark
cunt on a yacht
cunt under a pretty dress trying to hide from a cellphone camera

cunt of the week
cunt of the month
cunt of tomorrow

ex-girlfriend cunt
new girlfriend cunt
cunt that looks vaguely familiar, will haunt you

cunt like whoa
cunt like no
cunt, like, maybe get a labiaplasty?

cunt in white cotton, black lace,
doing its kegels, drunk on itself,
post-orgasm, post-modern, pre-med,
pre-second-wave feminism, pre-Playboy,
prenuptial, preternatural, post-coital

cunt for president
cunt for prime minister
cunt for PETA

cunt with a grudge

sepia cunt
adorable cunt
lonesome cunt

cunt right there in your bedroom

THE FIRST TIME WITH PAY-PER-VIEW

Her body was an ostentatious palace
where he broke all the furniture.

PHOTOGRAPH

You tell me to look into the lens,
which I think of as your mouth.
The air is heavy with appetite.

You adjust my head with two fingers,
brush the hair from my face,
tell me *part your lips,*
part your knees.

The woman you're watching —
What does she look like
and
did we both have you?

You like her, I know.
You'll develop her:
a bit of generosity.

COUNTRY DRIVE

The wheat fields wave
their cinders,

all the gold hurts my mouth.
Inherent in the repetition

of each passing plot is delusion,
mainly the figure of a woman,

not me exactly,
but a version,

the me that dies in the nightmare.
She has started to show up

in all the familiar places.

BEES

They cruise the windowpanes,
drone into autumn, sup on wallpaper vines,
their feet sanding
the bedroom sills. Antennae stalk

my body as they make
their honey
from blooms they find,
unknown to me.

They scour the kitchen floor.
I scare easy, make a peach pie.
We eat together on the back porch.
They comb my mouth,
fly out when I speak.

Before I leave this place, I'll
douse the hives at night.
I'll spray and spray and run,
turn to watch the bodies pour out.

THE COUNTY

i.

The light lies on the lake for so long
it might never leave, until
black gathers along the clothesline and beneath your hair,
climbs up the deck stairs.

ii.

When I was a child
dusk made me homesick for a resemblance.

Before the film flickered on at the cottage drive-in
I'd whirl on the playground carousel and hope to die.
The movies brought us other selves,
my parents beside the car in lawn chairs,
their faces unavailable.

iii.

A bird slams the windshield.

It lives but leaves feathers.
I flick the wipers.

Yesterday, a fox flashed in front of my car
to cup a rabbit in its jaw.

ROTATE

This piano music
chills the blood.

I drink warm beer.

The static on this record is a past
I dance with.

You said no alcohol.
I did say that.

Exceptions.

On the phone
he still calls you "my dear."

Absent-mindedly.
But you pause.

I pause.

On auto, the record player
restarts itself

but I recognize it
as the dead in this house

rising to repeat themselves.

FREQUENCIES

The radio preaches.

I put my mouth to the speaker:
Who sent you?

Tell it lies
about the truths

I've never told.
I spin the dial,

love watching
the indicator coast

along that silver line, frequencies
marked like gas stations and rest stops.

I call the station and the DJ says
he worked country radio in Alberta once,

hated it, moved back. *Ontario's
the best*, he says. My mind swats

a fly and I hang up.
He plays the song

and my other rises
to take the floor.

LETTERS FOR YOU

i.

The men around here drive pick-ups.
I watch them coast from the fields
in the evening, windows down.

We lock eyes when I'm out running
and I plead, turn to see if a glance
is in the rearview.

Their bedrooms are elaborately
simple; I'm a girl in them.

Sauvage, that's what you called me,
but it's how I think of you, and it's the opposite

of their want, which can be fed.
Cruel though, how their damp sheets
promise a forgetting.

ii.

Forgetting.
Tricky, that.

We tried to do it
by moving away

from our past
and into a house together.

While you sleep
I walk around the empty rooms
with a blanket over my shoulders,

hoping to recover someone.
Not in the dining room.

Not in the study.
So I shed my clothes

and climb on top of you,
trying to find her.

iii.

Mid-morning walk.
You made observations
from your jacket:

how grave I was in my pretty hat,
how you'd always imagined

Anna Karenina looked like me.
I parted my lips but didn't say anything.

Don't be strange, you said.
Be strange, you said.

Back inside my mouth
fell open for your cock

like a string puppet's.

iv.

We stayed up
making purple-black flowers
bloom down the side of me.

We hoped the neighbours
would call the police
to stop us.

Someone, stop us.

v.

How quickly

we travelled
each other

in that other direction.

When you moved inside me,
we were astonished.

I think of it now as a grip
we could not remain under.

Here, there, a beauty returns —
one of yours —

I turn away from it.

THE MISOGYNIST

Every night she sits in the room with the big bay window, drinks
a beer, and imagines the city moving closer. She sees herds of
high-heeled women walking down County Road 2. She wants to
rip their heels off, throw rocks. She wants to hunt them. They
would run stupidly, she is sure, then, Jesus, she thinks, who am
I? and tilts her beer.

Now she paces and puts on a record of Soviet Army marches.
The noise fills the cottage and impedes her ability to listen
for intruders. She always listens for them. Men, she knows,
might be waiting outside her bathroom window, or maybe
her bedroom window, to climb in and rape her. All night she
can't sleep because of the men potentially waiting outside her
window: squatting, lurking, silhouette cut-outs like that kid used
in *Home Alone* to scare off the bad guys. Except these ones are
outside, not inside, malicious and silent, not laughing, dancing.

In the morning she brews coffee and goes out to her back porch
to meet the gardener, the first of the men to work for her. Later,
the contractor will come inside to fix the wall where it meets
the ceiling in the sitting room and she'll stand below his ladder,
hands on hips, and watch.

FATHER'S SON

I'll say it:
I am afraid
you'll end up like your father,
alone in the woods with a blonde

retriever. I watch him setting rock
in the mortar of the new cottage,
think of his hands on a woman's body,
how your mother's face was no stone.

He prefers this: still structures
leaning into autumn.
Gutting fish, stringing up deer to drain,
online dating with women he dismisses

as stupid. He wishes they were nineteen,
he says, he wishes for a daddy complex.

I swim in his lake,
track your movements on shore.

ASTROCOTTAGE

Crickets chirp
on the Jumbotron.

The animals are mascots
to your shotguns, to nature,

which is twenty-two here
and wearing a string bikini.

I saw a deer raising herself
from the meadow,

but it was a beer ad
about chugging cans

as cold as lakes,
it was a head

on the cabin wall,
it was the forest shuffling off.

SMALL CITY

When I lived there I roamed shopping malls
on lunch break. They advertised Katy Perry

was coming. I sat in Starbucks obsessing.
The university kids couldn't tell

but the men on their computers could.
I puppeted my arms for them, my mouth.

One followed me home through a snowstorm.
A snowstorm won't stop me!

It was a declaration of psychopathy, like my moving
was a declaration of psychopathy. And that word

declaration, an icicle glinting in the infrequent sun,
on one of those days I felt we were living

in a farmhouse,
dinner fresh from the oven,

snow a violence spun for us,
like fate was a thing we would die doing.

CURIOSITY

He entered every watering hole he ever saw on Queen Street.
He went for breakfast and dinner and coffee.

He entered greasy spoons and empty trattorie, bars
with signs like *White Magic Psychic*.

It didn't matter. He needed to eat.
He needed to know how it was inside.

She likes this about him. She imagines this is how
he feels about women. Their outsides

draw him; he is curious
about their taste and the way they feel,

the experience of them. She can understand this.
She can understand anything. She is sitting

at the back of a coffee shop
watching the barista smoke quietly on the stoop.

There is a sign on a balcony above him
that says *Vienna House Bakery*, she wonders

if that is what she would find in him:
oven-warmth and rising.

Her lover sees many storefronts
inside her. When he says,

"I would ask you to marry me
if you believed in marriage," the hope

goes out of her. His idea of it
is the diner in the Edward Hopper painting:

all our loneliness under a glow, the couple
just beyond reach, and the milkshake slinger

in his white hat, promising.

KING WEST: BRIAN

"Melissa will probably want to do something domestic
tomorrow, like go to Ikea."

Will she suck his cock today?
They make purchases together:
white mugs and shower curtains,

and he asks about the wine she's chosen
for their dinner party, and she goes on
wearing her dark-wash jeans

and when an explosion of colour suddenly leaps
from the fog between them, out from
that spot in her mind that is still hers,

still free from some ad on TV,
direct from the sparking edge of her teeth
she bares up from his lap,

he almost—just for a second—loses
his hard-on, lives inside the gentle
arch of her hand on his knee,
the horse-muscle of her neck.

TRINITY BELLWOODS PARK: GIRL

"Rachel! Your bush is showing!
You're not wearing any underwear!"

Her body leans into the grass
with its bright legs

and high-waisted floral jumper comeback.
She spreads her fingers around a Pabst Blue Ribbon

and lifts her face.
She doesn't know if she's an American Apparel

mannequin or a woman with
a body she's learning.

She wants every boy in the park, and none.
Yesterday she sat in front of the mirror

brushing her hair,
wondering what belongs to her.

She presents herself to the world
like an art show, different concepts

behind each look, hoping
the critics will elaborate.

Her last boyfriend
wanted it bare.

LIBERTY VILLAGE: SEPEHR

"Four girls masturbating together in a hotel room is so
unnecessary."

We broke for lunch,
chose sushi.
Do you find this California Roll sexy? I asked.
What I meant was: How do you forget?
Rice fell from his mouth.

I watched an interview with an ex-porn star.
They asked him to reflect on the difference
between porn then and now.
When I was working...
I remember being turned on to a point sometimes...
I would actually shake...I'd hate to see that go away.

They filmed him tending the garden
and cooking spaghetti for his wife.

We office back in to caption clip after clip,
Redheads, Blondes, Busty Brunettes.

LOVE, MONTREAL

It makes me wet to think of
the way your fingers touch objects —
coffee cups, corkscrews,
bike chains, and faucets.

You asleep quick, like a man who
works with his hands,
and the car headlights
from Rue Sherbrooke steal
across your face. Jesus,
even now, even still.

WOMEN-ONLY BEACH, PORTO MARINA, EGYPT

Folds and folds of black cloth drop
and suddenly, a woman.

I watch from
my rented chaise lounge
as she runs to the sea
like any other pussy-on-stilts,
like me.

In the water she opens and closes her legs
to let the flow in and out and back to the cargo ships
with their working men and steel containers.

PRIVATE TOURS. ROME.

Campari breath,
glass of ice, rumpled
explorer suit.

When his wife leaves the table
he puts his hand on my arm,
leans to my ear...

Elephant, I mutter, and it's true.
He had pounded around the basilica
begging for peanuts.

His wife has a neck like a giraffe
and wears her hair in a chignon.
They have the miracle of money.

What? he asks.
But his wife is back
with a fresh cake of make-up.

LOWER FORMS OF LIFE

The trees and sky can be ripped away.
Behind them you'll find a peacock.
When his tail opens flames eat
what is left of the picture,

including the peacock,
whose feathers are made of a lace
my grandmother gave me
on my twenty-first birthday.

I put the lace around my thigh that year,
put on a white dress, and a man's head
appeared below, asking after the cake.
The people took pictures of my golden thighs
and we drank champagne with dark bubbles.

The bed trembled beneath me
and outside, snow fell furiously.
The position was lonely.
The ceiling cracks opened
and blood flew brightly.

A child with thrashing feet
sullied the blushing gates.
She came out greedy for air, screaming.
The doctor's hands choked her squirming body
and I decided to give her the one chance:
I told her everything would be visible
in the golden fleck of my left iris —
all there was to steal from me —
and her snail ear twitched
under my hot breath.

YOU AND I IN THIS HOUSE

i.

He might start an apocalypse in this body.

What body?

Mine.

ii.

Where are you?

Lying in bed watching our paintings melt,

watching the doors unhinge themselves.

iii.

In the morning, what do you do?

We sip coffee and break bread.

I read the commandments off his face
and compile a list I can slip in my pocket,
pull out to remind me.

iv.

His beard opens, eyes flicker.

He's an imposter.

No. This is spirits seeing
from their spot at the back of my brain.

v.

We need another line of salt.

For what?

The spirits.

vi.

I head for the grocer's at the end of the block.
The traffic signs are pornographic,
men linger in their back seats.

I climb in a Chevy and open my legs.

vii.

    Who is he?

No one.

A pair of blue jeans.

viii.

After, he talks to my belly button
as if it were a telephone,
orders room service: "pomegranates, please,
and a slice of moose meat."

    Are you okay?

No, none of this is mine.

ix.

My body comes
and kneels down to me.
I wish it would leave me alone.

But the cat at the foot of the bed,
his eyes on fire.

You're pregnant.

x.

How do you feel?

Like I can't remember my line.

He passes me the script.

xi.

How did we get here?

Where?

Here.

xii.

All night
it's only us two.

xiii.

And when day comes?

BEAUT

I'm neat in short-shorts,
or I used to think men thought so,
until I met you and your smartphone,
which you'd rather be ogling

than me neat in anything.
It makes me wonder if men looking
is just a routine, like exercise,
and how pathetic I am

to hope for and shine in it,
should I want it.
I rarely do.
Women file shining under

ACCOMPLISHMENT
Fuck accomplishment.
On a summer morning in short-shorts
I watch pallbearers carry a coffin

down a flight of church steps.
I sip my morning latte.
The guy next to me says, "It's a little early for this"
and I am supposed to agree

but I shake my head, imagine this:
all the mourners after, feasting
together. Is that beautiful?
At this bar in Sihanoukville:

young men on MDMA.
One of them looks at me
like I'm a piece of sky.
Then shuts his eyes.

There was a beach beyond that bar
and I sat on it watching lightning,
thinking beauty should mostly be
someone making that spectacle inside you.

INSTAGRAM

My lover's twin daughters
draw me rainbows.
I tape them to my walls,
where they startle me.

It's not enough.
I need rousing abstractions of myself,
the mirror is a failure,
and small hearts can't touch mine.

The nihilistic one loops her fingers
through my knit sweater,
says she wants to destroy it.
I'm about to board a plane.

The piece is more style
than functional, so I respect
her opinion. *I can see your point,*
I want to tell her,
but Dad beats me with *that's not nice.*

Shame springs from nice,
a prickly beast. So you heart everything,
like a dumb bitch. And you wonder
if real ever was
as the ground slips from under you.

VICTIMS

My man prepares elaborate dinners,
takes time with them, bends
over my plate at the table
with a lime or dash of salt.

Other women are aroused.
I've already had my hands up this skirt
(which I chose with malice),
a different colt in mind.

His children cut up construction paper hearts
for me in the basement of the art gallery;
it's psychological warfare. At home on the futon
they stretch their bodies over mine,

kiss me with mouths of small teeth.
I never should have agreed
to braid their hair or clasp their barrettes.
They check my eyes for imagination.

My ex reminds me in a telephone call
how I'd once leaned to his ear at a wedding,
the flower girl flouncing down the aisle —
We all love a little girl in a pretty dress.

BODY

i.

We live in my lungs.
You smoke.
You set up an armchair in the corner,

bring your books and newspapers, lean back,
read and exclaim facts about the fall
of empires and the decline of women.
On the back of a magazine

a girl poses in a dress, straps
slipping down her shoulders,
something moving under her

skin as if it knew
the place. It
doesn't. But

I know the blaze
in my belly: it burns
this conversation,
sends smoke up through my eyes and mouth.

ii.

There is another side to history.
In factories where dress threads come together
women hum to drown their hunger.

iii.

Art is a looking-glass.

I see myself in a painting, the one
in which the heroine's breasts are like bruised apples
and a shadow watches from the window.

The girl in the painting —
and the one in the magazine —
are, in a way, fucking us, filling us.

iv.

What you meant — when you mentioned
the decline of women — was
that empires nearing
the brink of collapse
make stars out of women's eyes.

WITNESS

I see this lady going door-to-door
with an armful of pamphlets.
I'd like to be that sure of anything.

At a funeral
my mother took me aside,
"I believe when I die I'm going up there."
She pointed to the stucco ceiling of the funeral home,
her other hand clutching a dry brownie
wrapped in a white doily.

"And all the people I love..."
she said it pleading-like, self-mocking,
too intelligent for God, like the rest of us.
As if I wouldn't want her to have that.

I want her to have that.
I sat next to a bouquet
on the car ride home,
its sick-sweet smell
like the thinning perms

that bobbed in the sparse pews.
I didn't know what to do
when they bowed their heads.
I kept my eyes on the bald minister,
who looked like '80s Florida,
and while everyone around me broke
down, I was on a plane to Miami.

MARGARET HANNAH

If I had a child, occasionally
I would stare at it
and wish it dead.

What would you want instead?
I would want to be gathering rain in my wheelbarrow,
boots on, thinking about the land spread out around me.

My grandmother had land
and she sat on her porch looking at it,
a well of rage in her. You don't understand:
she was happy. She was the happiest person I knew.

Her husband had flipped his truck one night,
beers in him, a death at the kitchen table,
the kitchen table was still there the next morning,
the woodstove was still there. His grave
is in the churchyard next door, she too
is there. Her mind went long before
her body. I did not grieve her flesh.

There's a road allowance to a hill
behind her house. I walk it,
stand at the top, walk back
to the house. Another family
lives there.

The heavy black furniture and oil
paintings. It was a lot to clear.

PHOTOGRAPH OF MOTHER

Your childhood yard
is an explosion of rust and weeds
backed by clapboard and peeling paint.
Poverty acid-dropped the landscape:

ragged chickens, desire
hung to dry, the men
drinking and picking fights,
the women worn right through.

Let's not get dramatic.
You still had tea parties in the garden
with paper dolls made from pictures of models
you'd snipped from Sears catalogues.

In your thinning dress,
squinting at the world
beyond your yard,
you willed better, saw the earth's

betrayal, all your ancestors tilling
to empty, digging up nothing
but grief. You would choose
subways and concrete,

teach kids to read, make paper money,
buy every packaged item
in the gleam
of the grocery store.

CANCER

My father's oncologist has two black sockets for eyes.

He hands me a lollipop after the diagnosis.
It's the colour of a wolf's tongue
and tastes of cold weather.
Your family's cancer comes from the moon.

A nurse pants as we crowd the hospital bed,
her teeth sharpening in my father's iris.

I see Orion lurking
and beg him to hunt this bitch. Too late:
the sun is coming on feverishly red.

THE COUNCIL

This house is full of skeletons.
They're bored:
throwing up dust on sideboards,
anxious in the unwashed sunlight.

They sit in a half-circle and face me,
encouraging the way I study each of their bones
by clapping their jaws.

I blink and see a calmer I
sitting alone in an empty room.

Her hair shines.
She is lonelier,
doesn't keep the company I do.

NOTES

In "Liberty Village: Sepehr," the interview with the ex-porn star that's referenced is from the 2012 documentary *After Porn Ends*. The quote comes from an interview with the late porn star John Leslie.

The Edward Hopper painting referenced in "Curiosity" is *Nighthawks* — not that it really needs introduction.

The Salvador Dalì painting referenced in section iii of "Body" is *Le Signal de l'angoisse*, which I first viewed in 2008 at the Scottish National Gallery of Modern Art (Modern Two) in Edinburgh, where it still hangs.

ACKNOWLEDGEMENTS

Earlier versions of some of the poems in this book have appeared in the *Malahat Review*, the *Edinburgh Review*, *Hazlitt*, *CV2*, and *Room*.

I couldn't have completed this book without the generosity, encouragement, and keen insight of a number of readers/editors over the years: thank you to Ryan Van Winkle (you continuously renew my fervour for this crazy thing we do), Linda Besner (I love you and you're brilliant), Nick Weaver (your friendship and belief in me over the past thirteen years has meant more to me than you know), Jennifer Still (you were a generous and gifted mentor), and Jeramy Dodds (thanks for good ideas, pushing me, passing this on).

Thank you to my editor, David Seymour, for his patience and persistence, and for a deep understanding of what I am attempting to do with poetry.

Thank you to my friend Kathryn Macnaughton for letting me use her brilliant, provocative artwork for the cover of this book.

To my parents, Barb and Paul—thank you for your unconditional love and support, despite your occasional fears I may end up a destitute poet. And thank you for being two fiercely intelligent, kind, and curious human beings with a profound love for literature.

To Kali'i Dixon and Rebecca Rappeport: your conversation and companionship in the last, often difficult year of writing this book were essential.

And to Clay: for a man who was once a stranger to poetry, you have become my best, most trusted reader. You are also my best friend, and I am continuously astonished at the depth of your love, support, and belief in me. Our thing has been wild and remarkable.

I also feel immense gratitude to everyone involved with the Al & Eurithe Purdy A-Frame Association. Without the time, space, and support I found at the A-Frame residency in the summer of 2014, this book wouldn't be what it is; Al Purdy and Prince Edward County are very present in these pages.

I'd also like to thank the Toronto Arts Council, the Ontario Arts Council, and the Canada Council for the Arts for their generous support in the writing of this book.

And to everyone at Goose Lane/icehouse: thank you for your dedication and hard work.

Katherine Leyton's poetry and non-fiction have appeared in numerous publications in Canada and abroad, including the *Malahat Review*, *Hazlitt*, the *Globe and Mail*, and the *Edinburgh Review*. She was the inaugural Writer-in-Residence at the Al & Eurithe Purdy A-Frame in the summer of 2014. A native of Toronto, she has lived in Rome, Montreal, Edinburgh, and Forlì and has made her living variously as a bartender, tour guide, porn writer, and library assistant. She now lives in Ottawa.